The Shock Story of Electricity

Anna Claybourne

Illustrated by
Kevin Hopgood

Reading consultant: Alison Kelly
Roehampton University
Electricity expert: Dr. Tom Petersen

Contents

Remember, electricity is really
dangerous. An electric shock can kill you.
So, never play with electricity,
and keep metal objects and water
well away from live electricity.

Chapter 1

Electricity everywhere

Electricity is all around us, making all kinds of machines work. But what is it? And where does it come from?

Computer

Stereo

Television

MP3 player

Iron

Electric shaver

Electric toothbrush

...and billions of people around the world have an electricity supply in their house.

5

Less than 200 years ago, though, there was no electricity supply at all – and no electrical gadgets either. So people used other things.

NOW

THEN

CDs

Musical instruments

Lightbulbs

Candles

Hairdryer

Sun

Toaster

Fire

There has always been electricity in nature. Lightning, for instance, is a giant electric spark. Back in prehistoric times, people could see how powerful lightning was.

But they had no idea it was a form of electricity – or that electricity could be useful to them. They thought lightning was a punishment, sent by their gods.

Chapter 2

Early days

In 600BC, an ancient Greek scientist named Thales made a surprising discovery.

Thales found that if he took a piece of amber and rubbed it with cat fur, the amber could pull things closer to it. It could even pick up light objects such as hairs or seeds.

The Greeks were amazed by the amber's power to pick up objects. They also found that, if they rubbed the amber a lot, they sometimes saw a little spark.

Thales and his friends had discovered a kind of electricity, although they didn't realize that's what it was. Some even claimed that if amber had such amazing powers, it must have feelings.

Later, other scientists tried Thales' experiment with different substances. They found that diamonds could pick up small things too.

Look what my diamond can do.

Hah! Wait till I try my copper.

But copper and other metals wouldn't pick up anything at all, no matter how hard they were rubbed.

Chapter 3
Electrical experiments

DOCTOR
W. GILBERT

Thales had made a good start, but
no one learned much more about
electricity until William Gilbert,
over 2,000 years later.

Gilbert lived in the 1600s. He was Queen Elizabeth I's doctor, but he was more interested in magnets than medicine.

In his spare time, he studied magnetism and tried out Thales' experiments with amber.

Excuse me! What about your royal patient?

Like Thales, Gilbert saw that rubbing amber gave it a pulling force. But he realized this wasn't quite the same as a magnetic force. So Gilbert named it *electricity*, from the Greek word for amber, *elektron*.

Soon, other scientists were doing their own electrical experiments. An American named Benjamin Franklin thought that lightning was an electrical force in nature. In 1752, he decided to prove it.

He believed that Electrical Fire – his name for lightning – could travel through a metal object such as a key. But he had to make sure the lightning reached the key, so he set up an experiment with a kite.

First he made a kite with a metal spike at the top.

At the bottom of the kite string he tied a key.

Then he flew the kite in a thunderstorm.

It worked! Electricity flowed from the clouds into the kite and down the wet kite string to the key.

When Franklin put his finger near the key on the end, he saw a spark.

It looks like the spark you get with amber. It's electricity!

By the way, you should never try this yourself. Franklin was lucky not to be badly hurt. The electrical force in lightning is so strong, it kills people.

From his kite experiment, Franklin came up with many of the words used with electricity today.

A substance that allows electricity to travel through it, such as metal, is called a _conductor_ and conducts the electricity.

The tingling – or stronger pain – people feel when they touch electricity is an _electric shock_.

A _charged_ battery stores electrical energy that can be released, or _discharged_.

battery

Franklin also invented a lightning rod or lightning conductor — a metal rod fixed to the highest point of a building.

The rod runs all the way to the ground.

If lightning strikes the building, the electrical charge is carried harmlessly down the rod into the ground.

The next electrical breakthrough came in 1786. Italian doctor Luigi Galvani was busy working when something incredible happened.

Galvani was studying a frog's leg, which was lying on a metal tray. When he touched it with his knife, there was a spark and the leg jumped.

Argh! It's alive!

BOINGGG!

"What was that?" Galvani wondered. Could there be some kind of electricity in the frog's leg?

Galvani's friend, Alessandro Volta, had another explanation. He believed that if you put something wet between two different kinds of metal, electricity flowed.

Galvani had two different metals — the tin tray and the steel knife.

Like all animals, the frog's leg was mostly water.

When he touched the frog with his knife, electricity flowed through the leg and made it twitch.

Volta tried putting one coin on top of his tongue, and a different kind of coin under it. He felt a tingling. That was electricity too!

So he built a stack of metal discs, made of copper and zinc, with thin cardboard soaked in salt water between each one. This became known as a Voltaic pile.

Copper disc
Wet cardboard
Zinc disc
Wet cardboard

When he joined wires to the top and bottom of the pile, electricity flowed between them. Flowing electricity is called an electric current.

Today, we use batteries that work in a similar way, made from copper, zinc and a special fluid instead of water. If you attach wires to a small battery, then attach a bulb to the wires, the current makes the bulb light up.

6-volt battery

Copper wire

Bulb

Electricity flows through the wires.

Electricity flows from the battery to the bulb and back, making an electrical circuit.

Galvani's idea about electricity in the frog's leg wasn't completely wrong. There *is* electricity in living things.

Yum! A fly!

Electrical signals carry messages from the brain to the muscles to make them move.

Some animals even make electricity in their bodies to use as a weapon – as Alexander von Humboldt discovered when he studied electric eels in 1808.

Ouch!

Chapter 4

Useful electricity

Just think what we could do with this power!

Once people knew how electricity worked, and how to make it, they started thinking about how to use it. All kinds of useful electrical inventions began to appear.

The most important inventor was Michael Faraday, who worked on electricity in England in the 1830s. Faraday was particularly interested in how electricity and magnets could work together.

He put a magnet in a dish of mercury, close to a wire with an electric current flowing through it. The wire moved in a circle around the magnet.

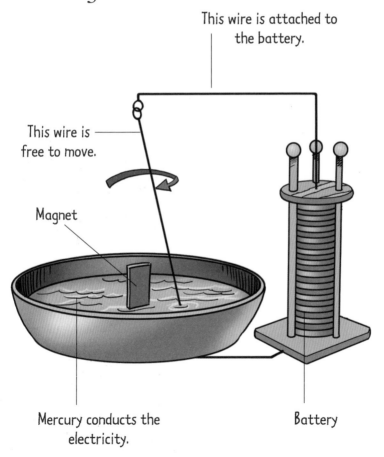

This wire is attached to the battery.

This wire is free to move.

Magnet

Mercury conducts the electricity.

Battery

Faraday's experiment led to two very important inventions – the motor and the generator.

A motor turns electricity into movement. You can see how it works in a modern electric fan.

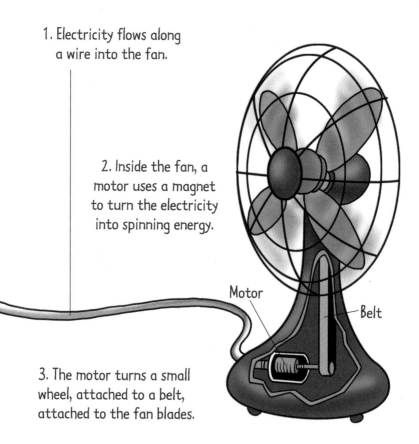

1. Electricity flows along a wire into the fan.

2. Inside the fan, a motor uses a magnet to turn the electricity into spinning energy.

Motor

Belt

3. The motor turns a small wheel, attached to a belt, attached to the fan blades.

There are motors in all kinds of electrical appliances today.

In a breadmaker, a motor makes a paddle turn around to mix the dough.

A motor spins CDs inside a CD player.

A motor makes the drum turn in a washing machine.

There's even a tiny motor in an electric toothbrush.

A generator works in the opposite way to a motor. It changes movement, such as the turning of a windmill, into electricity.

Wind makes windmill blades spin around.

The generator turns this spinning energy into electricity.

Then the electricity is carried away along power lines to be used.

Generator

Power lines

Most of the electricity we use is produced by generators. They can be driven by wind, water, gas, steam or nuclear power.

Other scientists working in the 1830s noticed that wires grew warm when electricity flowed through them. And if fine wires were coiled tightly together, they got very hot indeed.

As electricity flows through the tight coils, its energy makes the wire heat up.

Tightly coiled section of wire

Electric current

In the 1850s, inventors used this discovery to make the first electric heaters and stoves. Today, electric fires, toasters, kettles and irons all work using tightly coiled wires.

In 1809, Humphrey Davy – an English scientist – invented the first electric light. He made a strong current jump across a gap between carbon rods. It formed a glowing arc, so Davy called it an arc light.

The arc gave off a brilliant light.

Arc lights were used for decades. The problem was that they used up masses of electricity. They were smelly and smoky too.

A German, Heinrich Goebel, invented a basic light bulb in 1854. His bulbs burned for up to 400 hours.

In a lightbulb, electricity flows through a narrow, coiled wire called a filament. It heats up and glows white hot.

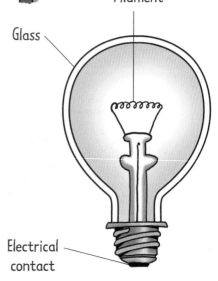

Filament

Glass

Electrical contact

Soon, inventors were designing their own bulbs. In 1880, American inventor Thomas Edison made a safe, long-lasting bulb that people could use at home.

Over the years, inventors came up with more and more electrical gadgets.

Telephone
– 1876

Vacuum cleaner
– 1903

Sound amplifier
– 1907

Television
– 1923

Electric shaver
– 1929

Electric blanket
– 1936

But at first these could only be used by the very few people who had electricity supplied to their homes.

Chapter 5
Electrifying

When streets and houses are set up with an electricity supply, it's known as electrification. In 1879, George H. Roe formed the first electricity company in San Francisco, USA.

We'll supply your electricity for just $10 a week!

Thomas Edison opened his own electrical power stations in London and New York. Wires from his power stations carried electricity for thousands of light bulbs.

Ooooh!

Aaah!

Whole cities could now be lit by electricity – indoors and out. On December 20, 1880, the first electric streetlights in New York were switched on, along Broadway.

But Edison's wires couldn't carry electricity very far. He was using "Direct Current" or DC electricity, which always flows in the same direction around a circuit.

The wires heated up as they carried the electricity, wasting energy and losing power.

The longer the wires, the more power is wasted.

So, in the 1880s, an inventor named Nikola Tesla found a way to make another kind of electricity, "Alternating Current" or AC. The current switches direction 50 or 60 times a second, and can carry electricity over long distances without losing too much power.

Before long, a businessman named George Westinghouse was building AC power stations. Edison was furious.

AC electricity is dangerous!

In 1890, AC electricity was used to electrocute William Kemmler, the first person to be executed by electric chair.

Despite Edison's worries, AC worked so well for supplying houses that it soon replaced DC. Today, most of our electricity is AC. It comes from power stations that convert energy from coal or gas, water, wind or nuclear power, into electrical energy.

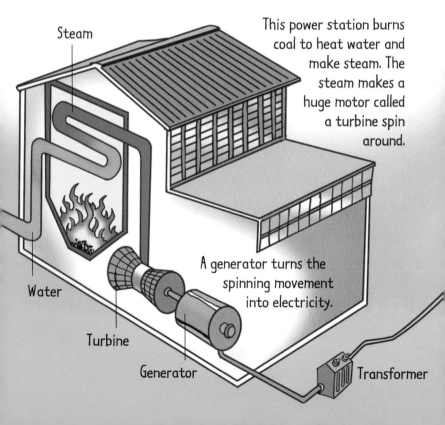

Steam

This power station burns coal to heat water and make steam. The steam makes a huge motor called a turbine spin around.

A generator turns the spinning movement into electricity.

Water

Turbine

Generator

Transformer

The electricity is carried around
the country through power lines and
thick cables.

Cables carrying
electricity

A transformer takes
electricity from the
cables and sends it
out to local buildings.

Underground cables
bring the electricity
to your house.

Inside a house, the cable is split into smaller wires arranged in circuits. These go all around the house, behind the walls.

On each circuit there are power sockets where you can plug in machines or appliances. When you plug in a lamp, for example, you add another loop to the circuit.

Electricity flows from the socket through the plug... along the wire... through the bulb, making it glow... and then back down the wire to the socket.

A switch lets you connect or break the circuit. This turns the lamp on and off.

Electrical wires are made of metal because it carries – or conducts – electricity well. The wires are then covered in plastic, which doesn't conduct electricity. Instead, it keeps the electricity safely inside.

Chapter 6

Electricity today

The modern world depends on electricity to keep going. Many people use electricity every day, and you can buy thousands of different electrical gadgets.

Every year, scientists come up with amazing new inventions that use electricity.

Surgical robots can carry out long, difficult and delicate operations.

"Smart" ink can store an entire library of books on a single page.

Cars can adapt to road and weather conditions.

The most important electrical appliances we use today are computers. The very first computers were built in the 1940s and they filled entire rooms.

Now millions are made every year – some small enough to fit in the palm of your hand.

Inside a computer, there are thousands of tiny electronic circuits called microcircuits. Electrical currents carry signals around them at lightning speed.

Close-up of a microcircuit

Using the signals, computers can store and process all kinds of information, from complex mathematical calculations to pictures and music.

Computers control all kinds of things – such as planes, trains, traffic lights, bank machines and cash registers.

Millions of computers linked together make up the Internet. People rely on the Internet to send and receive email messages and access useful information from all around the globe.

But computers only work if they
have an electricity supply. Without
electricity, the world would grind
to a halt.

That's exactly what happened on
the East Coast of the United States
in August 2003. The electricity
supply went wrong and stopped.
Nothing worked. No one knew
what to do.

The 2003 power failure only lasted a day, but it showed how much we need electricity. At the moment, most of our electricity is produced using fuels such as coal, oil and gas. But we know these are running out.

So scientists have found ways to make electricity using energy from dammed rivers, sunlight, wind and ocean waves and tides.

But one big question remains. Can these methods make enough electricity for everything we use?

A safe electricity experiment

When Thales rubbed amber with cat fur and managed to pick up light objects, he had discovered static electricity. Here you can make your own static electricity... and pretend you're a snake charmer.

1. Put a plate on a piece of tissue paper and draw around it. Cut out the circle. Draw a spiral snake inside it, like this.

2. To decorate your snake, draw a zigzag pattern and eyes with felt-tip pens. Then cut along the spiral.

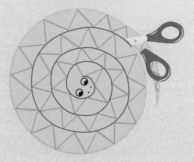

3. Rub a plastic ruler fairly hard and fast for half a minute with a sweater or scarf made of wool.

4. Then touch the snake's head with your ruler. Slowly lift the ruler. The snake should uncoil and rise up.

Static electricity enables plastic objects, such as this plastic ruler, to lift the paper snake.

Electricity safety tips

NEVER stick anything except a plug into an electric socket. The current in an ordinary socket at home can easily give you an electric shock strong enough to kill you.

NEVER touch bare electrical wire. This can give you a shock too.

NEVER unplug an appliance by pulling the wire. It might break. Pull the plug instead.

Be VERY careful with electrical appliances and water. Water conducts electricity, so only touch appliances with dry hands, and don't splash them or drop them in water.

NEVER fly kites, model planes or balloons near power lines.

If you ever find a fallen power line, STAY AWAY FROM IT. Go and tell an adult.

Edited by Mairi Mackinnon
Designed by Russell Punter
Series editor: Lesley Sims

Internet links

For links to some fun websites about electricity,
go to the Usborne Quicklinks Website at
www.usborne-quicklinks.com
and type the keywords *YR electricity*.
Please note that Usborne Publishing cannot
be responsible for the content of any website
other than its own.